Liberty

THOMAS M. GAULY

PHŒNIX

For Sarah and Julia

A PHOENIX PAPERBACK

First published in Great Britain in 1998 by
Phoenix, a division of the Orion Publishing Group Ltd
Orion House
5 Upper Saint Martin's Lane
London, WC2H 9EA

A CIP catalogue record for this book is available
from the British Library.

ISBN 0 297 84115 7

Typeset by SetSystems Ltd, Saffron Walden
Set in 9/11 Stone Serif
Printed in Great Britain by
Clays Ltd, St Ives plc

Contents

Are We Heading for an Authoritarian Century?

What will people write about our century? Will history books report that we championed the cause of liberty, or will they state that the battle between tyranny and liberty, between oppression and dignity, must be fought afresh? Will our children level accusations at us? Will they say that we have lived too much for the present and not enough for the future? Will they reproach us for carelessly squandering the gift of liberty? What will people write about our century?

Two world wars, more than a hundred military conflicts and civil wars, dictatorships and regimes of terror, not to mention the threat of a nuclear apocalypse: these have provided the twentieth century with its scenarios of horror. They have pushed the question of what people want to be free from to the forefront of intellectual and political discussion.

As our century draws to a close, the hope of living in freedom without state oppression has been realized for millions of people. Countries like Russia, Romania, Chile and Argentina, once feared as dictatorships which rode roughshod over human lives, have been transformed into democracies. Societies which were long shackled to authoritarian structures now present themselves as free societies. As the new millennium begins, 118 of the 193 states on this earth claim to be democratic. It seems as if the centuries-old struggle to achieve freedom and democracy can finally be consigned to the history books.

Yet it is absurd to celebrate the final victory of liberty.

What is more, it is absurd to think that the freedom of the West has been secured for ever more. Anyone arguing along those lines overlooks the speed and the depth of social change, which knows no limits. All the values of Western culture are in constant flux. This process is calling into question the existing forms of private interaction, individual lifestyles and general forms of behaviour just as radically as it is our existing view of the value of human life and the enforcement of law. The far-reaching nature of this transformation process is revealed by the debates which are being conducted in the West with mounting impatience. The same questions and the same issues are being raised in Washington and Los Angeles as in Vienna and Paris: the breakdown of traditional family structures and the yearning for spiritual orientation; the loss of social ties and civilised modes of behaviour; the decline of personal responsibility and the lack of authority of the state and its institutions.

Critics of the spirit of the age have already discovered the appropriate remedy for the spiritual crisis. They advocate a return to traditional values such as a sense of duty and responsibility, public spirit and solidarity. By contrast, we do not discuss our interpretation of liberty. We in the West believe all too strongly in the superstition that our liberty is adequately secured by means of well-equipped armed forces, democratic parliaments and functioning markets, so we refrain from carrying on such a debate. But it is deliberately overlooked that the Western interpretation of liberty has undergone a fundamental change in the course of the twentieth century and that our consensus on the limits to freedom is increasingly breaking down.

This fact will have fatal consequences for Western democracies. Like the major turning-points in thinking during the sixteenth and eighteenth centuries – the Reformation and the French Revolution – the demise of Communism, the triumph of electronic communication and the globalization of business signify radical upheavals for Western culture. This not only affects the way in which the West sees itself in intellectual and cultural terms but also the social cohesion within our societies and the competitiveness of our economies. These huge challenges produce upsets and trigger social conflicts. They make those people in particular feel insecure who feel that they cannot cope any longer with a world which is growing ever more complex and chaotic. This provides a welcome opportunity for demagogues and extremists who seek to abolish the liberties which are enjoyed as a right and to dismantle democratic institutions.

The 'new democracies' provide numerous examples in this respect. Even democratically elected leaders like Boris Yeltsin and Carlos Menem of Argentina by-pass their parliaments and rule by presidential decree by brushing aside the mechanisms of democratic control and promoting their personal advisers to important government posts. In most Asian democracies as well, citizens' liberties are severely curbed. On the other hand, notwithstanding recent setbacks, these states are demonstrating how to remain competitive despite ever more global financial markets and a harsher international economic climate. Is a new democratic and societal model developing here which can cope with the challenges of a globalizing world better than the Western countries can, given their fossilized democratic structures and their adherence to cherished privileges? Is the restriction of liberty essential for achieving political targets and for preserving competitiveness in the twenty-first century?

There can be no doubt that the 'illiberal democracies' (Fareed Zakaria) are to some extent attractive and fascinating for the West as well. Of course, nobody would like to exchange their level of prosperity for that of Russia or Argentina. But the claim that in such countries it is possible to use a firm hand to create law and order appeals to more than simply the politically unsophisticated. In virtually all societies in the West, signs of authoritarianism can be found, ranging from the protagonists of political correctness to the formation of an internationally organized right-wing extremist movement. Their leaders seize upon the loss of moral authorities and the profound insecurity of many people when faced with the political, technological and economic upheavals as the present century draws to a close.

The question of what we want to be free from will no longer be central to the twenty-first century. This is the painful lesson that the twentieth century has taught us. Intellectual and political debates will develop into a dispute on the exercising of freedom rights and freedom options. We will be confronted with the question of how we intend to use our liberty and whether we are prepared to subject what we understand by liberty to radical revision. Discussion on re-drawing the boundaries of personal and political freedom will take on crucial significance. The quality of our answers will decide whether it is possible to prevent the backlash against freedom or whether we are entering an authoritarian century.

Chapter 1
We Are Caught in the Freedom Trap

A century is drawing to a close. One might think that its drama and the course it has followed had been conceived by imaginative scriptwriters and seasoned directors from Hollywood's dream-factories. The century began with ideologies and revolutions, economic crises, dictatorships and wars. Ultimately, however, the good has triumphed over the 'evil empire'. The twentieth century: a fairy tale with a happy end?

This way of looking at it has its logic. The collapse of the Soviet empire and the worldwide demystification of its inhuman ideology signal a historic change in epochs. This brought to an end a development leading from the First World War to two major revolutions and their terrible systems of oppression, giving rise after the destruction of National Socialism and the end of the Second World War to more than forty years of confrontation between Communist dictatorship and free democracy. Yet the peaceful capitulation of the East has exposed deep-rooted problems which stretch far beyond the twentieth century. They make it hard to believe in Francis Fukuyama's happy 'end to history' because, immediately after the end of the Cold War, real war has returned to Europe. The massacres in former Yugoslavia, the shootings and the rapes, the concentration camps and the 'ethnic cleansing' in the Balkans, not to mention Russia's war in Chechnya, provide us with no reason to shout loud hurrahs as our century draws to a close.

In the USA and Europe, the long-term consequences of

the East–West confrontation are now emerging ever more clearly. For fifty years, we trained our spotlight on the East, constantly focusing on the powerful enemy across the Elbe. Every party conference speech of the Communist Party of the Soviet Union, every movement of troops in Poland, every five-year plan and every announcement of a new generation of atomic weapons systems determined the pulse rate in the West. The summit meetings in Washington and Moscow, the military parades on Red Square and the rigid faces of the East German border soldiers at Checkpoint Charlie were an integral part of life in the West, creating a deep-rooted fear of a sudden attack from the East. On both sides of the Atlantic, a gigantic machinery of destruction was built up and numerous wars were fought by the parties of either camp. A host of spies provided countless pieces of information, genuine and bogus, about the potential foe. Several times, military confrontation was on the verge of escalation. In this way, a life-and-death rivalry arose. Each side made propaganda exclusively for the 'successes' of their system and tended to present themselves as perfect and to reject as far as possible any criticism. Eventually, Communism lost, for even such a sophisticated propaganda machinery was unable to conceal the systemic shortcomings of Marxist–Leninist ideology and the perfect methods of oppression employed by its agents. The economic disaster suffered by the COMECON (Council for Mutual Economic Assistance of the Warsaw Pact states) members was all too obvious, the methods of the Moscow police state used against its satellites were too brutal and inhuman, and the economic and ecological costs of the nuclear weapons race were too high.

Although this contest between East and West developed into a military and economic confrontation, it remained in its core and by virtue of its origins an ideological conflict. At the heart of the intellectual and political dispute between the socialist dictatorships of the East and the liberal democracies of the West lay different conceptions of liberty. How much freedom does the human being need? How much freedom may, or indeed must, he enjoy within society and the state? And is there a basic right to human freedom which is inviolable? It was the different answers to these questions which divided the world into capitalists and socialists, into reactionaries and progressives, into friends and foes. For this reason, it was virtually inevitable that the demise of the Eastern bloc was sealed by the answering of this question. For it was nothing other than the striving for more freedom that led to the foundation of Solidarnósc in Poland in 1980, to Gorbachev's *perestroika* in the USSR, to the 'peaceful revolution' in East Germany and to the final removal of Communist rule in the eastern part of Germany. It was nothing other than the hope for more freedom that gave the people in Hungary, in Czechoslovakia, in Poland, in Russia and the other countries of the former Warsaw Pact the strength to persevere and the courage to resist.

With the end of the confrontation the West, too, faces major challenges, because it has lost one of its most important ideological and political anchors of stability and identity in the post-1945 period. Free from external political and military pressure, the West all by itself has to find a legitimation and a goal for its freedom for the first time since May 1945. The prophecy of Georgi Arbatov, the chief Soviet ideologue in the Kremlin, is being fulfilled. In 1989, he threatened the West for a final time that 'We will do something terrible to you; we will take away your enemy.'

Whether Arbatov's curse will find fulfilment will depend

above all on whether the West is able to make use of its 'new freedom'. For the West has also embarked upon a dangerous development over the past five decades. Since it believed that its freedom was being increasingly threatened exclusively from outside, by the arms and propaganda machinery of the Soviet Union, its conception of freedom degenerated into a defensive ideological tool. The political rhetoric of the West came to be dominated by a conception of freedom which derived its supreme legitimation from warding off the enemy to the east. As a result, though, political debate on freedom became taboo. Anyone who started to talk about the loss of freedom in his own camp was soon suspected of having been indoctrinated by Communism and of being completely on the side of the enemy. In this way, the Western conception of freedom was cultivated on the political stage into an ideology, while at the societal level it was increasingly robbed of its meaning. Half a century of prosperity, growth and security has turned the freedom of the West into an everyday affair. In the meantime, it has degenerated into something quite arbitrary.

This has led the West into a freedom trap. As we have been obsessed since the end of the Second World War with defending freedom on our external flank, our conception of freedom has undergone a fundamental transformation inside our Western democracies, spurred by the self-realization ideologies of the 1960's, a confidence in technological progress and the dominance of economic processes. Exaggerated individualism has eroded the limits of individual freedom and has led to freedom becoming boundless. A destructive conception of freedom has developed which breaks down both the individual's abilities to communicate and to form binding relationships and the social cohesion of society. As a result of an egocentric interpretation of freedom, we are beginning to turn freedom against ourselves.

Society and politics become the tools of a collective egoism which is beginning to gnaw away at the social foundations of the free democracies. Only a few years after the demise of our enemy, it is becoming ever more apparent that the West is no glorious victor, but rather a sick patient. Mounting criminality and violence, the proliferation of fundamentalist groups, the erosion of social cohesion and the crisis of the family are just a few of the symptons of the West's sickness. Despite material affluence, despite the freedom to travel and ever greater opportunities for consumption, substantial anxieties persist, accompanied by a lack of orientation, dissatisfaction and decadence. We have overcome our arch-enemy, the 'oppressor of freedom', but it seems that we cannot be happy about this victory, for we do not have much idea about what to do with our freedom.

The desire for intellectual leadership and the search for values is correspondingly great. All the Western news magazines, from New York to London and Berlin, report week by week on the ever more urgent quest for virtues and values. In the USA, a group of political scientists, sociologists and philosophers formed in the eighties have been developing new models of living together on the basis of Western values. The communitarians criticize above all the rise in the number of people who refuse to accept their personal responsibility for the community as well as for subsequent generations. They call for more responsibility towards others, public spirit and tolerance. They urge the individual to show more commitment and the readiness to become involved; they advocate a return to long-established family values and a life in small, manageable circles. Alasdair MacIntyre laments the loss of virtue and the inability of our societies to resolve central moral issues such as abortion, war and violence in a general consensus. He proclaims the end of enlightenment and calls for a return to Aristotle's theory of virtue. Michael Walker, Amitai Etzioni, John Rawls, Charles Taylor and others stridently demand a debate on the moral foundations of Western societies. All of them champion the primacy of values and an 'active society' which defines new goals and develops visions on the basis of its intellectual convictions.

It is indicative that, simultaneously, intensive discussions on the same topics are being conducted in Europe as well. Numerous newspaper articles are devoted to the 'Transformation of Values' and an increasing number of bestsellers are being sold, such as Neil Postman's *The Disappearance of Childhood* or *Das Buch der Tugenden* ('The Book of Virtues') by Ulrich Wickert. For in France, Germany, Italy, Spain, Switzerland and the United Kingdom there is now a stronger focus on one topic: the imperceptible development within our democracies away from the values, ideals and origins of Western culture. In unison, critics call for more public spirit and solidarity, more self-initiative and sense of responsibility on the part of citizens. Debates of this kind have long found their way into the political sphere. The German Chancellor Helmut Kohl was the first head of government in the West to proclaim a 'spiritual and political change' when announcing his legislative programme in 1982. Several years later, George Bush and John Major discovered 'family values'. Hillary Clinton has written a bestseller that appeals to the moral feelings and sense of responsibility of Americans, and after his election victory in May 1997 Tony Blair also stressed that he wanted to put Britain morally back on course.

Yet the appeals of such politicians will be to no avail.

The call for more responsibility and public spirit will pass unheard. After all, the debate on values represents only the outer shell of a phenomenon which goes much deeper. The debate focuses on the core element of Western culture, namely liberty as the spiritual basis of our values. If this spiritual basis is not discussed, the crisis of values will likely to become more acute and the craving for spiritual orientation will grow even stronger. Authoritarian leaders and their slogans will gain more adherents and use the freedom trap for their own ends. This would prepare the ground for an authoritarian century.

As they enter the third millennium, the democracies of the West face their greatest challenge, for the struggle to secure liberty is taking on an entirely new appearance. It is not weapons or military strategies which need to be used to defend it but rather convincing arguments and democratically legitimated authorities. This fight for freedom will prove to be much more difficult than the Cold War, not only because it is fought with different weapons, but above all because we have to seek the enemies of freedom inside rather than outside our societies.

We should learn from the uneven history of the twentieth century at least that there is no such thing as a status quo of values; there is no certainty. No culture, not even that of the West, is safe against a relapse into barbarism. The disastrous history of Germany between 1933 and 1945, a cultured nation, which had produced such leading intellectual spirits as Kant and Goethe, Beethoven and Bach, should serve as a warning example here. Our values are in a constant state of flux. The concepts remain the same, of course, but their content varies. Since we have constantly looked at their exterior alone over the past fifty years and have assumed that the content would be preserved intact, we have fallen into the trap.

Chapter 2
At the Heart of the West

Anybody who laments the change in values, therefore, should note the change in the meanings which we assign to language. After all, the way in which we communicate with one another and the content which we assign to concepts is a yardstick for measuring the spiritual condition of our culture. At this point, Western societies are exposed to a threat. We do not do enough to reach agreement on the central concepts of our social life and as a result we are increasingly talking at cross-purposes. In this way, we are losing not only our ability to indulge in individual and social communication, but also the very values on which our social life is based.

Who would deny that over the past five decades the definition of the words faithfulness and tolerance, partnership, sexuality and family has changed radically in Western industrial societies? Yet, since this is the case, the societies of the West ought constantly to examine their central concepts and review their consensus with regard to them. We have to ask ourselves whether we accord to the concepts and the central values on which they are based the significance which is due to them for ensuring a social life in freedom in liberal democracies.

Is there such a thing as a hierarchy of values? Is it possible to distinguish between central values and those which are less important? Do not all values have equal significance? There is no doubt in my mind that values have varying degrees of significance for our social life in liberal democracies. There is a hierarchy of values. At the centre of these values stands the idea of freedom. This is the core feature of the West. From this value all the others are derived, since it is only on the basis of freedom that they take on their profounder meaning. Public spirit and tolerance, responsibility and respect can become real only if they are founded on a certain understanding of liberty. Anyone who, for example, allows himself to be guided by an egocentric definition of freedom which does not respect the freedom of others will never be able to act responsibly. Responsible action is possible only if the freedom of one person does not impinge upon the freedom of the other.

In the course of the history of the West, liberty was given a special interpretation as the prime value of the liberal democracies. From it, all the other values of private and public life such as equality, solidarity and justice are derived in the form of secondary values. Consequently, liberty is the focal point of our constitutions. It represents the task and the goal of all actions undertaken by the state. The preservation and securing of freedom counts as the supreme goal of democratic constitutions and of their organs, not least of the West's armies and of Nato. For the inner development of our societies as well, it is imperative that freedom is secured. All democratic parties and institutions of public life, including the media, must serve this goal.

The intellectual roots of the Western idea of freedom stretch back to the beginnings of philosophy in the Ancient world and under Christianity. It derives its ethical and religious significance from the picture of humanity projected by the Christian West. It is the picture of humanity as having been made in God's image and of the earth as the creation of God. It is fundamental to this interpretation that all human beings are equal before God. From this notion there developed the insight that all human beings are equal. Contrary to all ideological misinterpretations, this does not imply an egalitarian levelling, but rather the belief that all human beings, regardless of their skin colour or race, their nationality or religion, their social status or their sex, possess the same dignity. In this sense, the freedom of human beings is always bound up with their equality.

According to this definition of freedom, each person possesses the same inner freedom and the same right to his external freedom. Inner freedom comprises the intellectual and spiritual dimension of human life. It constitutes the ethical self-determination of human beings, their ability to assume responsibility for their own lives, and is directed towards the individual and collective goals which each individual can strive to achieve. It comprises those values which provide human beings with an orientation and a yardstick for their moral behaviour. By contrast, external freedom refers to protection against bodily harm, the freedom from material dependence, from institutional tutelage and violence, from war and the threats posed by natural forces. The Western view of human beings, therefore, is holistic. It comprises both human beings' capacity for freedom and its limits. As the human being is not the creator but rather the created, he is fallible and his abilities and talents are limited. As the human being is free by nature, he is capable of guilt in the moral sense; at the same time, though, the human being is qualified and endowed with the ability to assume ethical responsibility for shaping the world. So both egoism and altruism are laid in our cradles!

It took a long time for this idea of freedom to become the core feature of the West. Over the centuries, it has been subjected to many philosophical, theological and political interpretations; it has produced political systems and triggered bloody revolutions. No other civilization has been so shaped by the centuries-old turbulent struggle to attain the individual's rights to freedom as Western culture has been. All the great revolutions and resolutions were devoted to securing and protecting freedom. The Reformation sought to secure the freedom of Christians and the independence of religious confession and conscience; the so-called Glorious Revolution was committed to the division of power and the introduction of laws to protect freedom; the French Revolution aimed to enforce political and social freedom for all estates and all social classes; Humanism and the Enlightenment championed the freedom of man and his subjective role, as well as the ethical commitment of the individual towards the commonwealth; the Declaration of Independence of the United States of America focused on the freedom and security of its citizens; the constitution of the United States guaranteed the sovereignty of the people under the rule of law; the General Declaration of Human Rights by the United Nations on 10 December 1948 was dedicated to respect for and protection of the basic freedoms of all people.

After the defeat of National Socialism and the end of the Second World War, a community of democratic states committed to freedom and peace arose in Western Europe, Canada and the United States. Its basis was provided by the definition of liberty that is rooted in the underlying ideas of Greek philosophy, Roman law and Christian ethics and in the teachings of both Humanism and the Enlightenment. After the experiences of two world wars and the confrontation with the European totalitarianism of the twentieth century, the Western community of states sought to protect the rights of its citizens to be free internally and externally: the right to express opinions freely, to enjoy freedom of conscience and religious freedom, the right of the individual to develop freely in society, commerce and the state. The ethical foundation for implementing this notion of freedom was provided by the bourgeois virtues of Western societies, such as respect and the sense of duty, diligence, honesty, loyalty and family values. On this moral foundation, the idea of freedom became the intellectual and political centre of the West after 1945 and also served as an ideology for defending the West against the Communist dictatorships on the other side of the Iron Curtain: the freedom of the West stood in opposition to the lack of freedom of the East.

In the meantime, the concept of freedom has developed in many directions. For liberalization has destroyed not only our appreciation of the inner connection between freedom and control, but also our awareness of the limits of individual freedom and thus the responsibility of the individual for society. With reference to neo-Marxist theories, freedom was claimed to be the total satisfaction of natural needs and the elimination of all forms of bourgeois order and domination. As a result, the self-interest of the individual became the focal point of public interest, particularly since the keyword 'emancipation' increasingly made freedom into the vehicle of personal interests and less and less the commitment towards other people and institutions. The outgrowth has been the emergence of a culture of 'dutyless rights'. Freedom serves as a polemical concept for anyone seeking to realize their individual interests.

Thanks to this 'popularization', Western culture has tended to become more libertarian and the idea of freedom has undergone several grotesque redefinitions. Today the 'right to freedom' is claimed for all kinds of things. It is used to justify abortions and street blockades alike. Above all, though, freedom has become the symbol of consumption, the supreme rationale for legitimating the smoking of cigarettes, for the cross-border mobility of money and the unrestricted visual consumption of sex and violence on television. Not least, the advertising industry has played its role in harnessing the idea of freedom for the most abstruse things. Lottery enterprises talk of the freedom which can be bought with the lottery ticket; banks and other financial institutions offer 'great freedom' through the acquisition of shares or credit cards; companies motivate their workforces with slogans such as 'competitive edge, freedom, success'. In the political domain too the concept of freedom has degenerated into a meaningless everyday word, which is used to justify not only the general use of seat-belts in cars but also the military presence of the Americans in Vietnam or Nato troops in the Gulf War and in the Balkans.

These examples demonstrate that not only the interpretation of freedom but also the consensus about what freedom means has undergone a transformation. For this reason, it will be all the more important in the decades ahead to achieve a shared interpretation of freedom again which can serve the West as an intellectual compass – despite the differing interpretations of freedom which have always existed. If we fail to do so, we will discover one day that our talk about the freedom of the West has become hollow and empty. For the loss of concepts is followed by the loss of a common language. As ancient Babylon found out, the absence of a common language gives rise to the threat of disorientation followed by the danger of decline.

When the Nazis came to power in Germany in 1933, they eliminated step by step the language of freedom. They provided new content for concepts like freedom, fatherland, community, duty and family. This was the start of the revaluation of values and the strategy for the road to dictatorship. In his film *Schindler's List*, the American director Steven Spielberg presents an impressive example of the danger to freedom posed by the revaluation of language. The film narrates the life of the German entrepreneur Oskar Schindler, who manages to rescue several thousand Jews from death in the concentration camps. When Schindler learns one day that the employee closest to him who shares his secrets is to be deported to a concentration camp, he tries to reassure him:

Schindler: I'll make sure that you get special treatment if you are sent to Auschwitz.
Employee: I hope you don't mean by special treatment what people are saying.
Schindler: Do we need a new language then?
Employee: I fear we do, Mr Schindler.

The West today is not faced with the threat of a Nazi dictatorship. But the mortal enemy of democracy, the disintegration of freedom, does not require a right-wing or a left-wing ideology, nor the threat from an outside enemy. The superstition that our culture is indestructible and the debasing of our language will suffice. Language is the medium which enables us to understand the world. We see nature, society and human motivation not as they actually are but as our language allows us to see them. It is the foundation of our culture. For this reason, it is not immaterial how we treat our language and what our central concepts are used to denote.

Chapter 3
Where Is America?

The world power America is destined to play a key role in the search for a new interpretation of freedom. Spurred by its missionary zeal, the United States developed into the intellectual and political beacon for other nations of the free West after the end of the Second World War. The Statue of Liberty in New York harbour does far more than extend a welcome to the land of unlimited possibilities. It symbolizes the Americans' yearning for peace and liberty.

Economic growth, military supremacy, technological progress, social cohesion and widely spread affluence lent American democracy quite early on the attraction of the 'American way of life', which was felt far beyond Western Europe and beyond the Iron Curtain. Presidents such as John F. Kennedy, Richard Nixon and Ronald Reagan liked to be celebrated in the capitals of the world as the most powerful politicians of our planet. At the same time, they were regarded as the noble knights of the twentieth century who were fighting for the good against the 'evil empire' (Ronald Reagan) in the age of atomic weapons. In the name of freedom and human rights, American troops were not only stationed along the Iron Curtain but were also fighting in virtually all continents, constantly prepared to extinguish what was once the greatest threat to free people, the danger posed by Communism.

However, while the USA developed into the most important world power in the fight against Communism, the foundations of its social and political system began to crumble. Drugs and alcohol, corruption and scandals, crime and violence in the major cities all destroyed the glory of the American empire. Watergate and Vietnam symbolize an America whose faith in itself is deeply shaken. Although the rivalry with the East united the country's forces internally for a long time and directed the focus of attention abroad, hardly had the external enemy been defeated before the enemies within the ranks at home emerged more boldly than ever. The attacks on the World Trade Center and the bombings during the Olympic Games in Atlanta are brutal proof of this.

Americans were hardest hit by the Oklahoma City bombing. It was not only a nine-storey building in the Mid-West that was destroyed, but above all the belief in the invulnerability of the American nation. America felt itself threatened in its very being; its self-confidence as a world power was profoundly shaken. Symptomatic of the reaction to this attack was not only President Clinton's aggressive speech, in which he declared in an emotion-laden voice on the day after the bombing that those responsible would be tracked down, but also the search for the terrorists, which initially concentrated on Muslims. Yet, as was shown later in Atlanta, those behind this dreadful massacre were neither Communists nor Arab extremists. They were US citizens.

If we look back on the period from 1985 to 1995, we find an increase in extremist violence, exclusively geared to the realization of radical political and moral positions. In January 1995, for example, a terrible massacre occurred when militant opponents of abortion shot at close quarters two female employees at two separate abortion clinics in the North-east of the USA. Five other people were seriously injured. Previously, numerous demonstrations had taken place, involving physical attacks on the police. A growing number of people are calling for radical laws in order to bring about a moral rebirth of America. At the same time, criminal gangs are forming. Primarily, they deal in drugs, women and certain types of consumer goods which they have stolen. Such developments cast a light upon the spiritual condition of American society, which is characterized by mounting radicalization, and the readiness to indulge in violence and crime.

America's prisons are overflowing as a result. Statistically speaking, the Southern states have the largest per-capita prison population, of 4.5 per thousand inhabitants. Yet even more alarming than the absolute number of prison inmates is the rate at which their total is growing. In 1980, some 500,000 Americans were serving prison sentences. In 1997, more than 1.5 million people were in prison in the United States. Texas is the state with the most rapid growth rate in its prison population. In 1996 alone, 28 per cent more people were incarcerated than in the previous year. The second-highest expansion rate last year was registered at 20 per cent in Alabama. Experts estimate that, if things go on like this, by the year 1999 America will have as many people in the care of its justice authorities as it has students registered at universities.

William J. Bennett, former US Secretary of State for Education, detects ever more signs of decadence in America's societal development. Quite soberly, he notes that the rest of the world no longer sees in America the 'shining city on the hill', but rather a society in decline, with exploding crime rates and social diseases. Joseph Heller, one of America's best-known authors, published a novel in 1994 which deals with the social and political developments at the start of the twenty-first century. Symbolically, he gave his book the title *Closing Time*. Heller does not believe that there is any way of solving America's problems. He writes: 'we have reached a point at which the opposing social forces field whole armies of cold-blooded street-fighters. Everything is falling apart, seems doomed to decline.' There are more than a few observers who attribute the condition of America to its economic and social development. They point out that the discrepancy between rich and poor is becoming even greater and at the same time the commitment to values and democracy is waning. The statistics seem to prove such critics right. Fifteen per cent of the US population live below the poverty line, fewer than 50 per cent participate in elections – basically only the affluent vote. In 1991, 36.6 million US citizens were unable to afford health insurance. As a result, 16.6 per cent of the population were not insured in the event of illness.

Although the American economic spiral has been turning more and more quickly for years now, the real wages of the mass of the population have not felt the benefit. Only the upper 20 per cent have seen their incomes advance by 15 per cent and more. The average weekly wage of a gainfully employed person, however, amounts to about $390; with this amount, an employed person can buy just about the same as with the $345 which he was earning when the upswing began in 1990. The real incomes of Americans who did not graduate from college have remained flat for the past twenty years. A further 40 per cent whose vocational qualifications can be described as no more than mediocre live in fear of losing their jobs. For most people, the hopes of achieving a steady increase in living standards have been dashed. While the US middle class is having to accept a decline in its economic situation and many at the lower edge of this social class are having to hold down several jobs simultaneously in order to support their families, there is a growing number whose share in the affluence of the global economic power USA is limited to the services provided by public soup kitchens and private support for the poor. Robert Reich, Labour Secretary in the first Clinton administration, believes that in the foreseeable future American society will vote for a form of capitalism different from the present one. For the first time in the history of the United States, parents are having to tell their children, 'You won't have it as good as we have had it.'

The economic situation of the American middle classes is mirrored in the financial situation of the public sector and the over-indebtedness of the US goverment. In the winter of 1996/7, for example, President Clinton was obliged to send thousands of public officials home because the government was no longer able to pay their salaries. Even if we consider this measure to be a political move on the part of the Republicans who wanted to dictate the terms to President Clinton with the aid of their majority in the House of Representatives, this highlights the American problem. The most prominent example of a highly indebted city in the USA is Washington DC. In 1997 the American capital was over $500 million in the red. Public services constantly break down due to the acute lack of funds. Refuse is no longer collected and occasionally the traffic lights cease to function during the rush hour. In the summer of 1996, there was a drinking-water scare when dangerous *coli* bacteria proliferated in the water pipes. A headline in the US magazine *Time* compared the situation in the dilapidated US city to that in the Third World.

These days, irrational forces are rampant; and the faith in the workers of miracles and religious leaders who claim to hold the key to success is growing. They preach spiritual leadership and economic blessings to gullible Americans.

Hundreds of thousands of US citizens have drifted into abstruse religious sects. The border line between recognized Churches and sectarian soul-catchers seems hard to draw. It is not surprising, therefore, that in early 1997 thirty-eight people took their lives in order to reach a 'higher place' in a UFO following the comet Hale-Bopp. This was the largest-scale mass suicide to date in the history of North America. Experts fear a wave of such tragedies in the years ahead. Just like a thousand years ago, when the West was shaken by apocalyptic fantasies of destruction at the start of the second millennium, experts believe that there could be orgies of violence around the year 2000. This is possible against the background of a society whose problems are considered soluble by an ever decreasing number of its members and which at the same time is losing its consensus regarding the intellectual and moral yardstick upon which it is founded.

Yet the widening gap between rich and poor, the spread of crime and the intellectual disorientation have left behind deep scars not only in the United States but in European societies as well. There has been an increasing growth in the number of opinions, interests and convictions. Pluralism is now more diverse than it has ever been. This is positive because it is an expression of our freedom. At the same time, though, fundamental patterns of orientation and accepted social features of our culture such as mutual respect, the readiness to help, the sense of responsibility and duty have all been lost. The advocacy of unlimited possibilities for self-realization, the cult of the individual and the spread of an uninhibited emphasis on consumption have transformed the individual's right to freedom into the claim to seeing his individual wishes fulfilled. The ability to enter into long-term relationships is impaired, a development which is dramatically documented by, among other things, the number of broken relationships and marriages.

A glance at the relevant statistics makes not only the scale of the interpersonal tragedies evident but also the speed with which the transformation of values is taking place. Whereas in 1972 of all twenty-four-year-olds about 63 per cent were married, this had turned into a minority of 26 per cent by the start of the 1990s. This trend runs counter to the intentions and wishes of most, since practically 80 per cent of the under-thirties say that they would like a lasting marital relationship and wish to start a family. However, in Germany and other Western societies, 30 per cent of all marriages on average end in divorce. In some regions, young people go their separate ways within one or two years of their honeymoon. Frequently, it is the children that suffer. In Germany alone, more than 92,000 were left 'orphaned' as a result of divorces in 1992. In Denmark, only one household in four consists of a married couple with children. At the same time, fully fledged single-person societies have developed in recent years. In Frankfurt, Munich, Paris and Milan, over 50 per cent of households consist of only one person.

In the days of America's founding fathers, the family was the place where personal experiences and values were passed on intact to the next generation. By the end of the present century, however, a radical transformation has taken place. In many American households, a much more influential source of education and socialization exists alongside the family in the form of television. In Europe as well, television viewing has undergone a truly explosive development since the 1960s. The total broadcasting time of Europe's largest public law television channel in Germany (ZDF) has much more than doubled since 1964, rising from 105,000 minutes per year to 278,000. The introduction of cable television and private channels has led to a perceptible increase in the consumption of television. This affects all age groups and social classes. TV viewing today begins at the age of three and expands step by step. A 1990 survey into the media behaviour of girls and boys in eastern and western Germany in the 6–13 age bracket shows a steady increase in television viewing in the 6–7-year-old age group up to the 12–13-year-olds. Children in the 6–7 age group spend an average of 70 to 100 minutes a day sitting in front of the TV screen. 12–13-year-olds 120 to 130 minutes. The average viewing time for adults is 170 minutes per day.

The extensive consumption of television and of other mass media such as video, radio, magazines and the popular press has destroyed cultural traditions. For one thing, the strict separation between the public and the private has been almost completely destroyed. For another, the taboo zones of the intimate sphere and of violence have become the everyday fare of our media society. Modesty and discretion, privacy and taboo are being radically called into question because the publicizing of matters by the medium is considered to represent a value all in itself, in keeping with the motto: what is not public does not exist – life is only life if it is reflected in the media. It is not only children who are exposed to these slogans of never-ending entertainment. Adults too are becoming TV addicts and are submitting themselves to the subtle seductive mechanisms and powerful influence of the medium. Here as well there is not only a loss of social communication; other habits and attitudes are altered too. Neil Postman's superb essay on public discourse in the age of the entertainment industry rightly draws our attention to the process of intellectual and political self-destruction which is bound up with excessive television viewing. The danger in this connection appears so great because we have at our disposal neither instrumental nor ethical criteria for approaching this medium in an adequate manner. For this reason, millions of adults and children are exposed daily to the spiral of sensations and violence which is systematically leading to an ethical truncation and moral brutalization of our societies.

Indicative of this trend towards a society lacking contours is the development in the American entertainment industry, which is increasingly becoming the protagonist of decadence and indifference. Brutality, sex and violence predominate in America's film industry to a hitherto unknown degree. Oliver Stone's *Natural Born Killers* created a scandal in Germany because of its obscene scenes of violence. In Ireland, the film was banned; in the United Kingdom, its launch was postponed indefinitely. Films like *Pulp Fiction* and *Killing Zone* followed, which showed torn bodies, bullet-ridden heads and running blood on the big screen. Unlike in the brutal films of the past such as *Rambo*, the cinema heroes of the late twentieth century have no motives for their violence. They murder for no reason. Good and evil have ceased to exist; the culprits emerge unscathed. The legitimation for such films is provided not only by their producers' thirst for sensation and the fact that these films prove to be box-office hits. They are legitimated above all by the moral indifference on the part of a large section of Western society. 'Be good. Be bad. Just be' was one of their most successful advertising slogans in recent years. Without intending to do so, it sums up the mental attitude which has gained ground in the 1990s.

In view of such developments, it is understandable that European countries are casting anxious looks across the Atlantic and are concerned that the social trends there could pose a threat to the political strength and determined stance of the United States. In May 1995, the International Institute of Strategic Studies in London claimed that the world lacked a strong leading power. The international political scene, it noted, was characterized by a diffuse feeling of impotence, and President Bill Clinton in particular showed a lack of leadership. In the view of the Institute, the only leaders who still had visions and stood by their convictions were the supporters of various forms of 'fanatical ideologies'. The weak leadership qualities of the American administration seem to reflect the crisis in society. The private affairs of the President and other high-ranking representatives of the administration are a part of this. In view of the intellectual climate in the United States, verbal radicalism such as Newt Gingrich's threat that, without a 'vibrant American civilization', 'barbarism, violence and despotism' would spread throughout the world no longer even sound arrogant. They show that some politicians in the United States are still not prepared for the twenty-first century; adopting a backward-looking position, they appeal to the past.

'The people feel extremely insecure' is how Thomas Mann described the state of American society from the Brookings Institution in Washington. James Thurberg, professor at the American University in Washington DC, says that the nation is searching for 'its identity'. Here he noted a 'marked swing to the right in the US public'. Politicians like Gingrich who seek 'renewal' openly assert that 'Our society is thoroughly sick. It needs a radical overhaul.' According to a survey run by *USA Today*, two-thirds of all Americans fear they may become the victims of violent crimes. Nine out of ten complain about ethical and moral decline. The majority of Americans believe that their country can move forward again by looking back into the past. This is the argument used by several states in order to reintroduce the death penalty. In 1997 it was admitted in thirty-eight of the fifty states of the USA. In Alabama, prisoners are chained together and made to clean public parks and bus stations again. In the mid-1990s, young men and women throughout the entire country publicly vowed not to have premarital sex.

In an article for an international weekly news magazine in 1995, Gingrich tried to explain why he believes that the USA is predestined to lead the world. He summed up in the following words: 'Using the tested methods of our past, we are mastering the future and are renewing American civilization. In this way, America's leading role is being strengthened and also its efforts to bring prosperity, freedom and security to humanity as a whole.' The face of America is altering perceptibly and it seems as if the scenario which President John F. Kennedy emphatically warned about during his visit to Germany in 1963 is becoming reality: 'Our freedom is in danger if we rest upon our achievements, for time and the world do not stand still. Change is the law of life.' Kennedy then added: 'And those who look only into the past will miss the future.'

As a result, uncertainty is growing about the ability of the USA to continue to take responsibility as the leading nation of the free West in the future, if the intellectual and moral forces that bind together the American symbiosis of wholehearted pluralism and national pride, the nurturing of tradition and multi-culturalism, wane even further. For not even the American nation is able to escape the centrifugal forces of a libertarian society, which may end in the situation probably best described by the Anglo-Irish poet William Butler Yeats in a poem dating back to 1919: 'Things fall apart, the centre cannot hold . . . mere anarchy is loosed upon the world.' The model nation of the West along with its pupils finds itself in an intellectual and political crisis. With some justification, *Neue Züricher Zeitung* asked on its front page, 'Where is America?'

Chapter 4
The 'Unholy' Market

It is one of the ironies of world history that Communism, while vehemently rejecting the market and competition, itself became the most important player in, and driving force behind, an unabating rivalry between the systems of East and West. At first, the contest between the market and central planning represented the attempt to provide theoretical proof of ideological superiority. Later the focus switched to political, military and, not least, economic predominance as well. It did not take long, however, for Communism to reach the limits of its economic potential. The free market was merciless and proved itself to be the relentless agent of a system which does not give moribund competitors a chance. The victory of capitalism cannot be denied. Since then, the globe has been ruled by a monopolist. The market is king; the rivalry between the systems belongs to the past.

However, as business became ever more global in character, a fresh critique of capitalism started to form in the post-socialist era. The core of this critique is the assertion that capitalism has arrived at its final frontier. Now that its major enemy has been removed, it is said to be condemned to ring in the end of its own history. The charge levelled against it is that, through its fixation on its rival, capitalism over the decades has lost sight of the immanent weaknesses of the West's social and economic system. The American social scientist Immanuel Wallerstein interprets the social and economic problems of the Western industrial countries – oversaturated markets, widening social gaps, overstretched welfare states and excessive government deficits – as the final phase in the long period of dominance of the capitalist economic system. He believes that the collapse of the socialist economic system also marks the beginning of the end of the age of capitalism, since over the centuries capitalism has degenerated into a system of profit maximization and exploitation. The American economist Lester Thurow points to the inequality of income and living standards in the industrial countries and asks how long Western societies can go on in view of such inequalities before the system collapses.

In order to understand the moral critique of capitalism we need to return to the beginnings of classical economics and the founder of free-market economics, Adam Smith. Unlike the mercantilists and the physiocrats, Smith emphasized human labour as the source of wealth. Productivity is increased through the division of labour. The value of goods is determined not by their use value but by their exchange value. The levels of wages, capital income and the basic rent, the three types of income, are determined by the market situation. Since Smith was basically a moral philosopher rather than an economist, he developed his theoretical writings around the picture of the whole man. On the one hand, he imputed to human beings the faculty of human sympathy; on the other, he recognized in them an unbounded self-interest, which he considered to be a natural urge of mankind. According to Smith, this self-interest is the driving force behind all economic actions and thus the motor of the market. Adam Smith's advocacy of the free market was accompanied by a double endorsement of freedom: the freedom of the individual and the freedom of society. Like all the great social philosophers of the eighteenth century, he was very keen to protect the individual against the tyranny of the state. He rejected an economic order that was manipulated by the state machinery because, in the final analysis, this curtailed the freedom of the individual and gave rise to a society which lacked freedom. He therefore rejected tutelage of any kind on the part of private institutions, which would restrict personal freedom through narrow rules and norms.

But how could it be ensured that the free society would also be a moral and just society? In three of his works, Smith refers in this connection to an 'invisible hand' which makes sure that work is distributed in a fair manner to the advantage of and in the interest of society. Yet we do not find concrete descriptions of this 'invisible hand' in either his *History of Astronomy* (1750) or in his *Theory of Moral Sentiments* (1759). Nor does *The Wealth of Nations* (1776) provide any concrete references. All the same, with this concept Smith established a myth in the capitalist camp: the ineradicable belief that ultimately the market will ensure a fair balance of interests. This marks the birth of an ethics of capitalism but also the origin of a historical misunderstanding. For although Smith himself did not place all that much trust in the 'invisible hand', given the tension that exists between sympathy and self-interest, it came to be interpreted in the course of history as a moral regulator ensuring that the market does not degenerate into an immoral institution. The popular interpretation is that the 'invisible hand' permits everyone to do whatever serves the good of the whole; what is more, through free competition, it is supposed to lead to a natural harmony between social and economic life. The outcome is a free society, constrained by only a few interventions on the part of the state, which takes its orientation from the values and goals of the *bonum commune*.

Two hundred years on from Adam Smith, it is becoming

clear that the market has unleashed a force which can no longer be controlled. In the course of history, it has increasingly transformed the traditional consensus on values in Western societies, promoting the unrestrained 'self-interest' of individuals and of organized groups. The market has performed a process of selection, according to strictly economic criteria: the strong are rewarded, the weak are punished. This lesson taught by the market resembles a kind of economic Darwinism. The result is the targeted selection of those who, true to the principle of self-interest, are able to assert themselves effectively against others and the social exclusion of those who are unable to meet the demands of the market to a sufficient degree. In the long run, the consequence is an unjust distribution of work, wealth and income. If we look at the USA, we find the following development. Between 1973 and 1995, gross domestic product (GDP) expanded by 36 per cent. However, the hourly pay of blue-collar workers and white-collar workers in non-managerial positions, representing the majority of the gainfully employed, declined by 14 per cent over this period. The entire increase in income during the 1980s benefited those in higher income brackets who account for roughly 20 per cent of the gainfully employed. More than 60 per cent of the growth in income went to top earners and a mere 1 per cent to those on average incomes. The United States is to the fore in terms of the widening gap between the upper, middle and under-classes. But the other industrial countries are marching in the same direction.

Many different examples testify to the success of the self-interest of the strong. One of them is the existence of powerful lobby-groups. Since the 1960s, efficient organizations, trade associations and unions have sprung up which are increasingly exerting a stranglehold on political activities and the state. Employees organize themselves against employers, the old against the young, those who have something to defend against those on the perimeter of society. In order to still the greed of the organized, politicians have piled up mountains of debt over the past twenty years and these will represent huge burdens for coming generations. At the same time, inflated government apparatuses, powerful bureaucracies and inefficient systems of redistribution have been set up. In Continental Europe, the share of government spending in GDP has surged as a result of the continual expansion of public sector borrowing. The financial debt of Germany, Europe's leading economic power, stood at DM833 billion in 1996. More than half of the country's gross national product (GNP) now passes through the hands of the government. The outlays on public assistance alone climbed from DM14.9 billion to DM31.8 billion between 1980 and 1990, and in the wake of unification they have reached DM52.1 billion (1997). In the mother country of the Industrial Revolution, the United Kingdom, the social welfare budget alone absorbs a third of all tax receipts. It has been about £3 billion higher than the limit set by the government for several years. In France, the ratio of taxes and social security contributions to GDP stands at 44.2 per cent, in Italy it is 46.3 per cent and in Sweden as high as 53.3 per cent. As wealth becomes ever more scarce, the struggle among the 'greedy' is intensifying. The motto here is that everyone is his own neighbour. This principle is applied both individually and collectively. It is not only within the framework of organizations and associations that interests are created. Individuals also try to use the community for their own ends. The consequence is illegal recourse to social benefits, tax and insurance dodges, and acts of theft. In themselves, these so-called peccadilloes are responsible for damage amounting to several billions of D-marks.

The dynamism inherent in our economic system has triggered a second far-reaching development: the predominance of economic thinking. One consequence of this is the revaluation of gainful employment in the second half of the twentieth century. Gainful employment has taken on the status of a surrogate religion. Whereas for many centuries work was regarded as a necessary evil in the high cultures of the West, as essential for securing people's subsistence, and only those were free who did not have to undertake any gainful employment, the market-economy system has forged a new definition of freedom since the nineteenth century: 'work liberates'. This statement, which was so cynically abused under the Hitler regime, seems to be finding its confirmation as our century draws to a close. We are addicted to work because, like no other activity, it brings us social recognition, personal satisfaction and material security.

For this reason the social–psychological impact of mass unemployment is profound. In Britain, Italy, Spain, France and Germany, unemployment rates climbed steadily between 1985 and 1995. In 1997, the ratio of the jobless (20–24-year-olds) to the gainfully employed was 39.8 per cent in Spain and 14.5 per cent in Britain. The OECD, which represents the richest countries of the First World, speaks of 37 million people without work. In the European Union alone, there are more than 18 million jobless. When apprentices cannot be accommodated on the staff of the companies that train them, when natural scientists and engineers with excellent qualifications fail to find jobs, and when middle-aged executives in middle management are politely but firmly asked to clear their desks, the very nerve of our world of work is struck. For individuals, unemployment means not only material disadvantages but also, and primarily, the loss of their feeling of being someone important; they experience a lack of social recognition and life loses its meaning.

The exaggerated emphasis on gainful employment has also led to the serious undervaluation of certain types of work which are of key importance for the survival of our free societies. The bringing up of children, the care of the sick and the aged, general housework and non-profit-making honorary activities rank in the lowest third of the West's scale of social values, true to the motto: anyone who does not earn is worth nothing. We are all dependent on these tasks being performed. But hardly anyone is prepared to undertake them for poor pay or, worse still, for nothing. This attitude destroys the sense of social responsibility and the capacity to form personal ties. One consequence is the loss of demographic equilibrium. As Western societies have failed to produce enough children since 1945, they have broken the unwritten contract between the generations and also the social contract which secured the balance between the gainfully employed and the recipients of social welfare payments. In Germany alone the over-sixty-fives will account for 26.7 per cent of the population by the year 2030, compared with 15.4 per cent today. One German in three will then be over sixty. Conversely, the number under sixty will contract by about a quarter. The ageing of society is not a problem confronting Germany alone. In the United Kingdom, France and the United States, the same process can be observed. Not without some scorn, therefore, Latin Americans, Africans, Asians and Arabs refer to us as the 'grey countries'.

James Buchanan, American Nobel prize-winner for political economy, has emphatically warned us to avoid the fatal combination of welfare states that can no longer be financed, a changed age structure, and the successes of medical science. He sees Western democracies caught between the mounting demands of their citizens and the foreseeable consequences of raising tax burdens further. If politicians respond to this dilemma by targeting merely the weakest social groups for their austerity measures and exclude the lowest-income groups from the social benefits provided by the community, he believes that discriminating welfare states would arise, which would cause an erosion of the foundations of parliamentary democracy. The British social scientist Lord Dahrendorf believes that there is increasing discrimination against, and exclusion of, today's under-class. In his opinion, future conflicts will therefore primarily be characterized by disputes about moral issues in our liberal democracies.

From the perspective of an Adam Smith, it was impossible to predict either the long-term impact of the selective dynamics of the market or the many-faceted predominance of economic thinking. Now, as we enter the twenty-first century, two more developments are emerging which cast additional doubt upon the effectiveness of the 'invisible hand': the significant increase in environmental damage and the globalization of markets. Adam Smith and David Riccardo assumed that a worldwide system of trade was possible, a worldwide division of labour, which would ultimately produce advantages for all nations. Instead, the national economies have developed in a very uneven manner. The pattern of winners and losers that exists in the national market is found in international competition as well. When controls over capital movements were removed and money markets were liberalized at the end of the 1980s, new rules developed and new players appeared, causing competition to become even keener.

Scholars of Harvard Business School are already talking

about the Third Industrial Revolution: the global diffusion of new technologies, new service industries, which are spreading from Europe and North America in the direction of the Third World. Each of the factors of production described by Adam Smith has become global, including the factor human being. By means of the new communications systems and the globalization of the factors of production, 1.2 billion workers in the Third World will enter the international labour market over the next generation. Roughly one billion of these workers currently earn less than $3 per day, while the roughly 250 million workers in the USA and the European Union currently earn around $85 per day. The experts believe that, once provided with modern technology, workers in the Third World are capable of producing to the same quality level between 85 per cent and 100 per cent of what their opposite numbers in the West produce at present. The Harvard scholars forecast no more than a slow expansion of real wages for employees in the Western world. Some wage groups may even see their incomes decline by as much as 50 per cent. This would have two consequences for the Western industrial countries. For one thing, the struggle to get work would intensify, as the worldwide competition for jobs will expose Western societies to an unprecedented pressure to rationalize, given their high pay and social welfare levels. For another, multinational companies would increasingly select their production locations on the basis of exclusively economic criteria, ignoring their national responsibility towards their 'countries of origin'. They would prefer to follow the major flows of funds which have gained in importance since the capital markets were liberalized.

While the consequences of globalization have to be viewed with concern and subjected to criticism, the positive side should also be clearly seen. In view of the West's saturated markets, globalization extends opportunities for economic growth and thus the chance to create new jobs, especially in the less developed countries. What is more, it increases the pressure on companies in the West to break down fossilized structures and bureaucracies. However, over the long term, the growth opportunities will prove to be positive only if there is no dramatic surge in the related ecological costs. The energy consumption of industries and households in the West already far exceeds that in the rest of the world. The creation of the greenhouse effect and the pollution of the earth, air and water have already reached dangerous dimensions, causing prominent scientists to predict an increase in steppe formation, floods and whirlwinds. Recent years have already witnessed far more natural catastrophes than were experienced in earlier years. The resulting damage is now on such a scale that the economic consequences are being debated alongside the ecological causes. Hurricane Andrew alone, which hit the United States in 1992, gave rise to insurance claims totalling roughly $16 billion. A glance at the insurance statistics confirms that Andrew was not a statistical aberration but rather the precursor of a trend. The average annual frequency of world-wide storms, for instance, has climbed from under one (in 1965) to five (1993). Since the 1960s, the damage done has increased tenfold.

In view of these developments, our economic and social system has to face a two-pronged critique. On the one hand, the market is under attack because its inherent dynamism makes it destroy values and virtues; as a result, it has promoted a 'turbo-capitalism' which fails to take account of the social and environmental consequences. This view is particularly endorsed by those circles in France, the United Kingdom and Germany who interpret poverty, social disintegration and environmental crises not as unintended by-products but rather as a logical outcome. The accusations culminate in the charge that, through globalization, capitalism has shed all responsibility for employment and democracy. In short, capital is losing touch with morality. On the other hand, the democratic welfare state has come under fire because it has apparently followed its Communist rival in systematically developing state control and planning. Moreover, it has led to countries piling up huge debt mountains, creating inflated bureaucracies and operating inefficient systems of redistribution. The market and its citizens, it is argued, have steadily forfeited their freedom. The most important tasks to be tackled by Western industrial societies over the coming decades have thus been outlined. They have to remain competitive in a context of globalized markets and ecological problems; at the same time, they must reinforce social cohesion and maintain political freedom. The successful handling of these issues will decide whether the West can retain its standard of living, but above all it will determine whether its democracies will be able to survive. For this to occur, the dynamism of the market has to be controlled by the values shared by its participants and also by the overall national and international setting.

Chapter 5
The Fear of Freedom

'With a slit throat into paradise' – 'Sudan's Islamists on the advance' – 'Muslim Farrakhan calls upon millions of blacks to take part in march on Washington' – 'Rushdie must not die' – 'New bomb attacks in Paris' – 'Islamic group GIA arm themselves' – 'Islam terrorist warning by authorities' – 'Muslim fundamentalists take up arms' – 'Bomb terror in the name of Allah'.

In the beginning of the nineties Samuel Huntington's thesis about the clash of civilizations came at just the right time. Having conquered its arch-rival, the West had had to wait for too long for a new enemy. Then this book by an American professor, who explained to us that the roots of future conflicts will no longer be ideological or economic but cultural, was published, and proved to be just what we needed. This was especially so since, for several years now, Arab-style Islamic extremism has been perceived as a threat by a number of politicians and journalists. As Huntington's bestseller was climbing the charts, a new and comforting certainty was nourished in Washington and Paris: that after a long wait we had finally found an acceptable successor to Communism in the form of Islam.

However, closer study of the new enemy proved to be less satisfactory. It was not possible to discover a new headquarters, similar to that in Moscow, from which our Islamic adversary received his instructions, nor was there a concerted propaganda offensive, let alone a declared Islamic war target advocating the destruction of Western culture. Could the clash of civilizations turn out to be a mere projection of the West? Not quite. After all, the confrontation between cultures has already become reality. It occurs wherever the West's conception of the meaning of life and lifestyle, of earning money and of enjoyment, violence and sex comes face to face with a religious definition of freedom. The clash occurs in a million places in the Near and Middle East, in Africa, in Asia as well as in Central and South America where Western television programmes are received by satellite and examples of the Western way of life meet with incomprehension, rejection and aggression. The few extremist groups that have pointedly declared themselves to be enemies of the West have done so not least because they feel provoked and insulted by the way in which the West interprets and pushes its freedom. These feelings, which are based on a deep-rooted fear of freedom, could one day provide the motivation for those who actively take up the fight against Western civilization.

Yet the 'fear of freedom' may become the driving force for a backlash against freedom which comes not from outside, not even from Islam, but from within the liberal democracies themselves. Its supporters can be found at all social levels and in all classes. They are people from the broad middle classes who for a broad variety of reasons could prepare the way that leads to an authoritarian system. Their movement in no way resembles that of a traditional political or socially homogeneous grouping. Nor is this a class conflict. Rather, it is a gradual movement, which at present is neither organized nor encouraged. Yet it is forming in the minds of those citizens who, like the Islamic extremists, reject the intellectual, moral and political condition of our societies because they feel nauseated, because they feel excluded or unable to cope with it, because they are afraid of losing what they have. They are comprised of an increasing number of anonymous people who do not yet possess the courage to stand up but who feel the growing desire to say 'No'. The Polish writer Andrzej Szczypiorski describes this movement, which he has noted in several European societies, in the following words: 'People are asking themselves today whether effective democracy can exist at all in a world of an unbounded, unintelligible and unordered variety, in which each opinion has its own legitimation and is disseminated by the electronic media. The consequence of such doubts will be the longing for authoritarian solutions.'

The excessive pluralism, which thanks to the media has reached a hitherto unprecedented level in our societies, appears to have become an end in itself. Our societies are changing at an ever greater speed. The most recent technological innovations in particular, especially in the area of communication by computer and data networks, are causing an enormous acceleration in the pace of life. As a result, the feeling of being under stress and of having no time have become widespread. Academic investigations reveal that most people feel that in their subjective experience everything is happening more quickly. In Europe, one person in four complains that life is passing by too quickly. According to a representative survey, Germans consider the lack of time and stress to be among the most significant causes of illness. To have 'no time' and nonetheless to be under pressure to take ever more decisions at ever shorter intervals seems to be the fate of the post-war generation. This is increasingly placing overly great demands on those who are not intellectually equipped to select out of the mass of opinions and bits of information that are offered those which are necessary and important in shaping their lives. At the same time, it disappoints those who need both moral and political orientation in order to find their bearings. For this reason, the longing for a fundamental change becomes stronger and stronger, as does the desire for authoritarian leaders. In Germany, France and Scandinavia, according to Szczypiorski, the prevailing atmosphere is that of waiting for something 'anonymous and secretive, which changes the fates of individual people and of entire societies'. People long for a firm order; they feel themselves incapable of taking continual decisions which they are compelled to do by the abundance of information, opinions, judgements, errors and even successes. Many reach the conclusion that two television channels would be preferable to a hundred. Life would then be simpler and less strenuous. Perhaps, some reflect, 'censorship' would not be so bad after all if someone were to decide what we need to know and what not.

Such thoughts are still taboo; they are aired in small circles but not yet in public. However, the movement is gaining in force. It is approaching its goal along different paths. In the USA, pseudo-religious groupings have sprung up which in public meetings impose upon themselves press censorship and corporal castigation. One of their offshoots, the 'Promise Keepers', are already active in forty countries and have over 200,000 supporters. Their members must pledge to obey the strictest rules of behaviour and they actively oppose abortion and divorce. As US examples underline, the fanatics among such groups do not even shrink from committing murder. On the whole, though, it tends to be a harmless movement which recruits its members from the traditional middle class. They consist of the old and the young, Americans, Germans, French, Italians and Spanish, all of whom champion a new morality, the family and the return to old values and virtues.

While this commitment certainly has its positive sides, and the international discussions on changing values also represent a positive sign that sensitivity still exists with regard to the intellectual and political crisis, we should be careful in forming an assessment of them. After all, the call for a return to former values can also entail the threat of a roll-back in social policy. Anyone pretending that we need only reach into the drawer of history in order to renew our societies consciously ignores the darker sides of past societal models. Of course, security, law and order can form the pillars of an order based on liberty. Yet they can also be abused to suppress the freedom of the people and to provide the legitimation for authoritarian rule. This is either not recognized in such circles or it is consciously ignored. The militia movement in the United States has 200,000 sympathizers. It is permeated with the romantic spirit of the days when America became an autonomous country. In California, disgruntled citizens are organizing themselves under the slogan 'Armed citizens for a responsible upbringing'; in Nevada, a group with the name 'Freedom at any price' is active. These militias represent the tip of a reactionary movement which includes sections of the white middle class. They appeal to moralists and weapon-freaks as well as right-wing radicals and citizens disillusioned with the affluent society. The declared opponents of these militias are liberals, atheists, spongers on the welfare state and representatives of democratically legitimated institutions.

In contrast to the growing religious-fundamentalist groupings and the paramilitary activists, the other forces advocating a backlash against freedom are hard to pinpoint. However, it is possible to describe five directions which might pave the way to authoritarianism. One movement is aimed at Western capitalism. In the USA and Europe, it is supported by those who are not prepared to accept without protest their declining level of affluence, who cannot find a job or must live in constant fear of losing theirs, who cannot afford any more social security and are consequently pushed to the edge of our societies, who reject the extension of economic thinking to all areas of life and live in fear of a global environmental catastrophe. This group of people see themselves confirmed by the sceptical theses of prominent scientists who criticize the impact of economic policy in the past and lament the predominance of economic thinking. They include such esteemed personalities as Ethan Kapstein, who in a *Foreign Affairs* article sums up his scepticism as follows: 'The world is possibly moving in the direction of those tragic moments when future historians will ask: Why didn't they react in good time? Weren't the elites in business and politics able to see the disruptions which the technological and economic development entailed, and what stopped them from undertaking the necessary steps in order to prevent a global social crisis?' Together with the American historian Paul Kennedy, Kapstein comes to the conclusion that there will be a backlash against the capitalism of the free market.

A second movement is directed against individualism and particularly against the emancipation of women. It is supported in France, Italy and Spain by those who lament the collapse of the traditional family and perhaps also by those who have grown up in broken families; who are suffering as a result of divorce and social isolation; who are not in a position to take the right decisions in view of the wide range of options; who regard the new relationship between men and women as a threat and want a restoration of the former positions of authority and domains of male dominance. They long for a return to the class-based society, where the hierarchy determines the position of a person, everyone has their allotted place and is given a moral order within the scope of which they are able to develop their personalities. According to Szczypiorski, many look upon such constraints as blessings because they take from individuals the burden of responsibility for their own fate. He claims that this 'flight from freedom' is by no means a novel phenomenon in our culture; what is new is that it is found 'everywhere' today. This movement is also directed against the media. It is supported by those who do not want to put up any longer with the flow of sex and violence presented by the media, who seek to protect their children from the consequences of media consumption, who are not prepared to finance the million-dollar salaries of the entertainment celebrities any more. Possibly Postman will be proved correct and this part of the movement will tend to remain small, as most of those involved are not even aware of the subtle mechanisms and consequences of media consumption. Yet the calls for censorship on the part of those who want 'sound information' and 'clean entertainment' will become all the louder.

A third movement is directed against the democratic welfare state. It is supported by those who are no longer able to share the blessings of welfare; who have to pay off the public-sector debt which the previous generation has piled up in order to please organized bodies and bureaucracies; who have to pay huge tax bills, levies and social security contributions in the full knowledge that, as they reach the end of their lives, they will hardly derive any benefit from these payments. But the movement will also be supported by those who feel discriminated against because they no longer participate in the welfare systems and they receive none of the benefits that are to be shared. And it is supported by those who feel unable to believe in the constitutional state any longer because it has become too unwieldy, too complicated and too bureaucratic; who have the impression that it is only possible to get justice if you have the money to pay for expensive lawyers. Even though there is no written law to that effect, there is an intrinsic connection between the social security which the state or a flourishing economy provides for its citizens and the stability of democracy. For this reason, James Buchanan believes that the Western democracies can survive only if their social welfare programmes continue to retain their 'general validity or quasi-general validity'. Otherwise, 'discriminating welfare states' would develop which would undermine democracy and lead to authoritarianism. In his view, Western democracies are increasingly moving towards the latter condition, largely without realizing this.

A fourth movement is directed against multicultural society. It is supported in the USA, France, Britain, Austria and Germany by those who feel cheated out of their jobs by foreigners; who suffer in some way from the integration of foreigners and from the crimes committed by the latter; who believe that they can escape the struggle between cultures in this way and interpret racism and xenophobia as cultural superiority. In Europe, there has been a significant increase in violent crimes against foreigners since the beginning of the eighties. In the United Kingdom alone, the police register a racial attack on a non-white citizen every twenty minutes. Between 1987 and 1997, assaults on blacks in the United States escalated. Symptomatic of the stronger aggression between races was the heated debate on *The Bell Curve*, which captured Americans' interest during the summer of 1995. The book advocates a new racial segregation into the stupid and the intelligent. Its authors claim that, for genetic reasons, blacks have a lower IQ than whites. Within only two months, 400,000 copies of the book had been sold. In European countries as well, a conflict potential has built up that should not be under-estimated, as those who are susceptible to such theories come from the right-wing extremist fringe that is well organized internationally.

A fifth movement is directed against modern technology. It is supported in Germany, France, the Netherlands and Italy primarily by those who oppose the peaceful use of atomic power and who, pointing to the Chernobyl catastrophe and other accidents, cast doubts on the safety of this technology; who believe that the negative repercussions of science and technology far outweigh their usefulness and consider the ethical issues raised by modern technologies to be insoluble; who reject any interference with human genes; who are no longer prepared to tolerate the over-exploitation of nature and the pollution of the earth, the air and water. This movement is principally made up of younger people who see themselves exposed to an all-embracing 'tyranny of progress' and allow themselves to be led by mostly irrational fears. In May 1997, a representative study appeared into the opinions and values held by young Germans in the 12–24 age group. The most important finding of this study was that 'the crisis in society has reached the young'. Eighty-eight per cent of young people believe that there will be fewer and fewer jobs but more and more jobless. Eighty-three per cent fear that violent conflicts are making life increasingly unsafe. In the view of 73 per cent, the economic crisis will get worse, and 63 per cent of young Germans have an even gloomier vision of the future. They believe that 'technology and chemicals will destroy the environment'. 'The lowest common denominator of these young people', writes one of the authors of the Shell study, 'is a massive sense of insecurity.' This, in turn, argues Ralf Dahrendorf, could add to the danger that a form of authoritarianism will develop, 'as a response to the moral dilemma of our society'.

The movements edging towards authoritarianism have still not found a political leader, let alone an organizational form at the international level. Supporters of the traditional extreme right, who are only too glad to work against the interests of freedom, possess the organization. Their networks extend far beyond the borders of Europe to the United States, Russia, South Africa and the Arab world. It is also possible to trace connections between Europe's radical right and the Ku Klux Klan movement in the United States or to the former South African World Apartheid Movement. In Austria, Belgium, Britain, Germany, Italy, the Netherlands, Spain and Sweden, there now exist tightly organized right-wing radical scenes with the accompanying press organs and propaganda forums, including electronic networks with the corresponding mailboxes. This right-wing radical scene draws its support not merely from neo-Nazis and white racists, but also from skinheads and the adherents of 'brown' esoteric ideas. On the political stage, this grouping is already reflected in legal parties such as the French Front National, the Italian Lega Nord, the Flemish Vlaams Blok and the Austrian Freiheitliche Partei Österreichs.

Last but not least, the fear of freedom has also reached those who after the collapse of Communism now live in Western-style systems, but for whom pluralism, competition and the market are entirely alien notions. According to a representative survey run in March 1996, the majority of people in eastern Germany are not ready to face the demands and strains of a system based on freedom. They do not feel at home in this economic and social system and are hoping for a 'third way', lying somewhere in between socialism and capitalism. No more than 31 per cent of eastern Germans said that free choice between several political parties was important to them, and only 13 per cent were in favour of the freedom to assemble and demonstrate. When the Czech Republic experienced serious economic problems in the early summer of 1997, support for the free-market system and the Civic Democratic Party sank rapidly. With some disappointment, President Havel declared that probably too much faith had been placed in the ability of the 'invisible hand of the market' to sort everything out. Similar feelings exist in the established democracies of the West. We should take them seriously and not denounce them as the work of enemies from outside our system, for such delusions will only blind us to the dangers within our culture.

Chapter 6
The Price of Liberty

As the end of the twentieth century approaches, the West is caught in a freedom trap. We have certainly overcome the most serious external threat to our freedom, dictatorship and Communism; but in the meantime an equally dangerous threat to our freedom has developed within our societies: a destructive interpretation of liberty, which has plunged the West into an intellectual and moral crisis. At its centre stands the individual who, on the one hand, can enjoy the truly unlimited opportunities for consumption and free movement, but, on the other, is increasingly suffering from the loss of social ties and lack of intellectual orientation.

Two everyday examples must serve to illustrate the dilemma of our multi-option societies and to pinpoint the subtle loss of freedom to which we are exposed. The first example describes the most popular daily leisure pursuit of millions of people in the United States and Europe. By the time they have had their evening meal at the latest, the TV is switched on. And it is all the same what the programme is. No matter whether it is a quiz show, a feature film, a news broadcast or a soap opera, whatever comes on is consumed – though with a clear preference for light entertainment. Three, four and more hours are spent in front of the set. Late in the evening, millions of television addicts fall exhausted into bed only to wake up tired out the next morning. Most of them do not even know what they watched the evening before. The second example is the collective buying craze which we witness in our streets, shops and stores. Music greets us from the holy halls of our consumer temples; customers are offered loans and the man on the street is promised that he can have what he wants most. Surrounded by this world of promises and seductions, you go out to buy for the sake of buying. Customers do not enquire about the cost/benefit aspect. As a result, entire industries live from the manufacture and sale of products whose processing and materials are so poor that their useful lives are bound to be short. Their only significance lies in their being purchased.

Both cases described above represent subtle forms of a collective loss of freedom. And it is cynical to argue that 'this is what people want'. For people neither want to be TV addicts nor do they want to have their hard-earned money take from them in return for some short-lived consumer articles. Yet because they are incapable of resisting the seductive mechanisms and the sophisticated sales strategies of the entertainment and consumer industries, they are just as addicted as the millions of sick people who are unable to do without such socially sanctioned drugs as alcohol and cigarettes. Will we have to impose bans on TV, consumer articles, cigarettes and alcohol and remove from people the right to enjoy certain freedoms?

At the start of the twenty-first century, these questions will be raised ever more frequently and will be generally discussed in Western societies. Politicians, preachers and demagogues will appear who answer the above question with a straight 'Yes'. An increasing number of people will become involved in authoritarian groups and parties. After all, the greater the lack of intellectual orientation, the more attractive authoritarian rhetoric sounds, offering remedies by means of simple solutions: safer streets through the restriction of civil rights, or morally intact young people through the introduction of flogging. Calls for censorship of the media will head the list of demands. They will give rise to bitter debates on the presentation of sex and violence, but also the freedom of movement in our society and the treatment of minorities.

In a second phase, the debate on freedom will lead to restrictions being imposed on the options for indulging in freedom. The first steps in this direction can be seen in the United States, where the ban on tobacco advertising and taboos on smoking have already become reality. However, the demand that the options for indulging in freedom be restricted will also have an economic impact. In particular, those who claim that market forces neglect social abilities and concentrate too much on the quantitative increase in options will call for limitations. The battle cries of the past century – 'More and more' and 'Nothing is impossible' – will draw criticism. In itself, the limited character of natural resources shows how wrong such slogans were. But the example of the 100 television channels and the millions of consumer articles also raises doubts as to whether the greater selection is matched by an improved quality of life, that is: freedom.

Discussion of restrictions on the options for indulging in freedom mark the start of the third phase of the controversy. They give rise to the question of how we intend to use our freedom. Economic transformations and ecological crises are calling into question the way in which the West sees itself. Above all, the notions of growth and prosperity are being subjected to scrutiny. As the quantitative notion of liberty is replaced by a qualitative notion, the conviction will prevail that we do not need an endless stream of new consumer articles, but rather better and better products with higher safety and quality standards; that we need products which use less energy and fewer raw materials. Recognition of this fact will change the West's interpretation of prosperity. A healthy and agreeable environment, health care which makes us secure against life's existential risks, and an intact set of relations comprising family, friends and neighbours will be the key components of a new concept of prosperity. It will be guided by recognition of the fact that we do not need the media and economic considerations to permeate our societies completely. What we do need, though, is more time for leisure and for tending our social contacts. Our new interpretation of prosperity has to be based on the recognition that our standard of living is no substitute for a sense of meaning in life, and also that the rejection of material affluence can mean an improvement in the quality of life – or, in other words, liberty.

In themselves, the intellectual currents of the 1980s and 1990s already point to the disputes and conflicts of the coming decade. Initially, the debate will be dominated by those who preach a return to authoritarian times and a curtailment of the rights to individual freedoms. The idea of freedom will have to be protected against such threats, and radical adjustments will be necessary. Communism proved to be incapable of achieving this even when faced with its own demise, because it lacked freedom. The democracies of the West are different. They have the opportunity to take their fate into their own hands. We have not yet reached the point of no return. We are still able to decide for ourselves about the transformation process. Yet we should do this soon. Before the protagonists of authoritarianism turn the general uncertainty to their own advantage, we must set about the task of renewing our societies from within. The strengthening of the capacity for freedom in the individual and the restriction of options for indulging in freedom are the price to be paid for securing our freedom. The most important condition for achieving this is the implementation of fundamental reforms in our social and economic systems. At the close of the twentieth century, the West is beginning a new chapter in the history of its liberty.

Further Reading

William J. Bennett, 'Getting Used to Decadence. Spirit of Democracy in America', *Vital Speeches of the Day*, 15 February 1994, pp. 264–69.

Amitai Etzoni, *The Active Society: A Theory of Social and Political Processes*, New York, 1968.

André Glucksmann, *L'Onzième Commandement*, Paris, 1991.

Rainer Hank, *Arbeit – Die Religion des 20. Jahrhunderts. Auf dem Weg in die Gesellschaft der Selbständigen*, Frankfurt, 1995.

Michael Kelly, 'The Man of the Minute', *New Yorker*, 17 July 1995, pp. 26–30.

Neil Postman, *Amusing Ourselves to Death: Public Discourse in the Age of Show Business*, New York, 1985.

Emma Rothschild, 'Adam Smith and the Invisible Hand', *AEA Papers and Proceedings*, vol. 84, no. 2, May 1994, pp. 319–22.

Andrzei Szczypiorski, 'Freiheit statt Pluralismus. Erste Früchte der letzten Revolution', *Frankfurter Allgemeine Zeitung*, 9 August 1995.

Lester C. Thurow, *The Future of Capitalism*, New York, 1995.

Fareed Zakaria, 'The Rise of Illiberal Democracy', *Foreign Affairs*, vol. 76, no. 6, November/December 1997, pp. 22–43.